TH Yourself® GRATEFUL

A DAILY "HAVE-DONE" LIST TO TRANSFORM YOUR LIFE

by
Nathalie Plamondon-Thomas

Published by THINK Yourself® PUBLISHING. www.thinkyourself.com

The author of this book can be reached as follows:

Nathalie Plamondon-Thomas: www.dnalifecoaching.com

ISBN: 978-1-7753653-0-3

First Edition: May 2018

FOREWORD

November 2016, and I'm sitting in the courtyard of an orphanage in Haiti, surrounded by a couple dozen kids. It is after dinner and they have changed out of their matching blue school uniforms into their after-school wear, which have been sewn from repurposed pillow cases. I had just had a cold 'shower', which was really two dribbles of cold water coming out of a deficient pipe that was duct-taped to the wall. The soles of my shoes still had remnants of the cockroaches I had had to chase away before entering the shower.

The 89 children in this orphanage in Grande Goave, Haiti were the 'lucky ones'. Certainly not because they did not have parents to comfort them and when they would cry at night, no-one would come; they would just cry themselves to sleep.

The reason they were the 'lucky ones' is because they had a second meal every day. For the other several hundred kids who lived among the six other schools operated by the Canadian-run Heart to Heart Foundation, the bowl of rice served at lunch was their only meal. A lot of families in Grande Goave cannot afford to feed themselves, especially in the months following a hurricane when their crops get completely devastated. They have to clean up the damage made by the violent wind and replant their gardens. Therefore, they rely on the support of this and other charitable organizations to feed their kids at lunch time, and it is very often that we see kids only eat half of their lunch portion and pass their plate over the fence for their parents to have the left-overs.

As they were surrounding me like they did every night after dinner, I thought I would help them by teaching them the "Circle of Excellence" (a technique of spatial anchoring you can learn in the THINK Yourself® series). The children were very attentive, as they love learning.

I was explaining to them how to draw an imaginary circle on the floor, step into it, and hold a power pose when you don't feel so great. It helps bring your mood up. One of the smaller girls asked: ''Nathalie, can you remind me again when we are supposed to step in the circle of excellence?''

I responded: ''You step in the circle when you don't feel great, when you are unhappy or when you feel sorry for yourself''. And the little girl responded with another question: ''But, aren't we happy all the time?''

I was stupefied. I did not really know what to say and realized these kids were just happy with what they had and that this technique was useless for them, so I responded: ''Well, that is right, you guys are happy all the time, so never mind, this technique is for us in Canada to use when we don't feel great.''

Then a small boy asked immediately with a surprised face: ''What? You are not happy in Canada? You have everything in Canada! Why aren't you happy?'' He came to me and grabbed my hand and gave me a big hug. All the kids joined and were all hugging me because, poor ME, we are not happy in Canada. I was bawling. Completely out of it. That really summed up the whole experience. I thought I was going to help them and in reality, these kids helped me.

I came back with a very true and profound realization: Happiness is not having. It is not 'stuff'. It is a feeling, it is being happy in the moment, in the process. The 89 orphans I hugged for two weeks have nothing. And yet, they taught me genuine happiness and a great deal about gratefulness.

This was definitely only going to be the first of many trips to Haiti as I am now getting ready for another trip with the amazing individuals that run the organization. I am also sponsoring a child, a beautiful boy, whose mother has disappeared, named Jean-Mary Youri.

INTRODUCTION

Hi, my name is Nathalie and I am grateful. I write books about neuroscience and brain programming. I love that stuff. I am fascinated by the fact that we normally know what we should be doing and yet, do the reverse anyways. A lot of readers who read my No.1 best selling books THINK Yourself® THIN and THINK Yourself® SUCCESSFUL tell me how much the system I shared in the books has completely changed their lives.

Now that they know how to set up their brain to be on board with their goals, they have the foundational layers to be ready to implement more of what they want into their life. While this book is only one fraction of the whole system that you learn in the THINK Yourself® book series, it is a great companion for a daily reminder of your goals and keeps you committed to living a true life.

I will introduce you to the astonishing powers of your brain and give you a simple daily tool to use to transform your life. You are awesome, and I can't wait for you to discover it.

It all starts by placing your order.

Enjoy,

Nathalie

TABLE OF CONTENTS

PART 1:
YOU ARE
AWESOME

CHAPTER 1:
YOU NEED TO HAVE
THE IDEA YOURSELF

The chief function of the body is to carry the brain around.
- Thomas A. Edison

Have you ever had a friend or a family member who shared with you that they had just come up with a fantastic idea? You looked at them stupefied, wanting to shake them and say: "Dude, I have been telling this to you for two months! All of a sudden, YOU just got this idea?"

Your brain is the most complex structure in the universe. Asleep or awake, it controls every moment, every movement and every thought of your life. It records what you hear, it distorts, generalizes and deletes information to create your model of reality. Somehow, we are all the same. We like to make sense of things ourselves, and we don't listen to advice. We only act on them when we can generate the light bulb ourselves in our brain. So just like we can take a horse to water but cannot make him drink, all the tips in the world will be useless unless you decide to do something with them.

This journal will help you to feed your engine with daily fuel. I will tell you why you should do so. I will explain each part in detail, then the rest of the book is yours to fill. Answering the specific questions that I designed in order to help you program your brain will condition you to generate the idea of doing what you want yourself.

A lot of my clients are now filling out these questions as a family every night. They all say at dinner what they did, how they chose to feel and what they are grateful for. This has even replaced the bedtime stories in some homes.

PART 2:

WHY SHOULD YOU BOTHER?

CHAPTER 2:
THE MOST COMPLEX STRUCTURE
IN THE UNIVERSE

Whatever we plant in our subconscious mind
and nourish with repetition and emotion
will one day become a reality.

- Earl Nightingale

THE LOGICAL MIND

We use our logical mind on the surface in our day-to-day. Your logical mind is the voice you hear in your head all the time. The one you use to make decisions. We give our logical mind lots of responsibilities and place lots of hope as to the extent of its power. The logical mind can process an average of between five and nine pieces of information at the same time. While you are reading this book, you are more likely also able to notice an average of seven other things.

Have you ever noticed when you are driving to a new address, as you come closer and start looking at civic numbers on the doors, you need to lower the volume of the radio in your car? Somehow, your 'five to nine' pieces of information juggled by your logical mind get filled up very quickly. As you are driving, with the foot on the brake/accelerator, noticing the red light ahead, the child about to cross the street and the weird guy in the car next to yours, somehow, doing all of this at the same time puts 'music' in the one-too-many category as you are adding 'looking at the numbers on the houses'. In light of this fact, knowing that we are restricted to handle only a few things at once, we may be tempted to dismiss the power of our mind.

According to the research of Dr. Raj Rahunathan Ph.D., we generate between 12,000 and 50,000 thoughts per day. [1] Unfortunately, up to 70% of these thoughts are negative. We wonder what is wrong with us? Why is everybody else successful except us? We tell ourselves we are probably not good enough. We think everyone is better and knows more than us. Sadly.

"Who would want to be your friend
if you talked to them
the same way you talk to yourself?"
- Unknown

Our logic might not be that great after all, right? The good news is that the voices inside your head can be reprogrammed when you discover and start connecting with the second part of your mind.

THE UNCONSCIOUS MIND

While the logical mind is busy talking down to you, the unconscious mind is busy working, listening and understanding everything, down in the deep structure of your own self. The unconscious mind can handle over two million pieces of information every second, (while our little logical mind was only able to manage seven, on average). Everything

---

1 https://www.happysmarts.com

you have seen, done, thought, heard or felt is organized in your deeper structure, waiting for your recall. Your unconscious mind considers everything. It reads all the signs and advertising while you drive to work. It hears every conversation around you, whether you are paying attention or not. It feels all the non-verbal signs that others are communicating with you without their knowledge. It captures all the 'behind-the-scenes' details that the logical misses. It takes all the info, it deletes, distorts and filters everything to create your model of reality.

Your unconscious mind has so much information for you. You have everything you need inside yourself. You got this. The problem is that people are not trained to think with their unconscious mind.

RELAX AND ASK YOUR UNCONSCIOUS MIND

When my clients and my friends want my opinion on what they should be doing, my on-going response is always: "It doesn't matter what I think. I don't have all the information that you have on this. You know exactly what to do, you are very smart and resourceful, and you will figure it out." I don't have their background, their experiences nor their values. They have to ask the only person that was there all their life; who noticed everything; who heard every conversation and even picked up on all of the non-verbal information not picked up by anyone else. They have to ask their unconscious mind. It knows exactly what to do.

The best moment to do so is at night before you go to sleep. Next time you need advice for something, before you get into bed at night, intentionally ask your unconscious mind to recall every piece of information you have on the subject and to give you a clear vision the next morning. It is essential to ask your unconscious mind to do this while you are profoundly asleep. (Otherwise, it could keep you up all night). You must specify that while your logical mind is recharging and getting long hours of rejuvenating sleep, you want your unconscious mind to work in the background so it can give you answers in the morning.

I often use this technique when I am not sure what to do, when I have a dilemma or when something is not working. It is usually that I am missing something. I send my unconscious mind on an overnight quest to give me answers in the morning. Sure enough. She always delivers. The other day, as I thought I had lost my driver's licence, after looking everywhere, it was keeping me awake and I could not fall asleep. I let my logical mind go and I asked my unconscious mind to look for it for me and to tell me where it was in the morning. By trusting my unconscious mind, I was easily able to fall asleep as I knew my driver's licence would be found in the morning. When I woke up, I suddenly had the urge to go scan a document that I had to send a client. When I opened the scanner to place the document to be scanned, my driver's licence was right there, waiting for me. I thank my unconscious mind.

When you send your unconscious mind on a mission, it keeps working for you in the background as you continue to live your life and while you get rejuvenating hours of sleep. It makes sure that things happen well for you. You can use your unconscious mind like you would use a personal assistant.

YOUR PERSONAL ASSISTANT

Your personal assistant inside your head takes notes and makes sure that everything that you say or think gets done. It's like having a waiter in your head, standing with a notepad and running to the kitchen to place your order. Whatever you think or say will get cooked by the chef and brought back to you exactly how you ordered it.

You have to be careful when you think and when you talk. Your personal assistant is always listening. If you wake up in the morning and look at yourself in the mirror and say: "Oh my! I look horrible! I look so old and tired! I am so over-weight," then you continue with your day saying to yourself that you feel so stupid, or inadequate, or you don't want to be stressed, and you hate rushing everywhere. You let the voice inside your head tell you that you are a failure and a fraud, and you even tell yourself not to forget this (maybe a folder you are supposed to bring to the office). All your brain can hear is: Horrible, Old, Tired, Overweight, Stupid, Inadequate, Stress, Rush, Failure, Fraud, Forget the folder, etc.

Close your eyes for a second and do NOT visualize Mickey Mouse wearing a yellow tuxedo standing on top of an elephant. Did you see him? Of course, you did! Even if you read: "Do NOT visualize Mickey Mouse...." Your brain doesn't process negation. You have to be care-ful! People sit in my office all the time telling me they don't want to be stressed anymore, they don't want to be fat, they don't want to be impatient with their kids and they don't want to be rushing all the time!

It is like they are telling their contractor that they want them to paint their kitchen 'not' blue. What do you want instead? Use your brain wise-ly, think and say what you want, not what you don't want!

Are you the person who is always saying: "I am terrible with names." Who decided that you are terrible with names? Who made the call? As you say that, you place an order to forget their name.

Some people say: "I am a morning person" or "I am a night owl." They conditioned themselves to be that way, and they believe it. If I need to stay up late, then I am an evening person, and if I need to get up early, then I tell myself that I am a morning person. I can be both. Whatever serves me. If a belief is not serving you, change it!

THE CHEF KNOWS HOW TO COOK

Sometimes, we undervalue our worth. We feel that we have to restrain our demands to what we know. We don't allow ourselves to dream too high because we don't know precisely how to get there.

Take the example of the waiter awaiting your order at the restaurant. When you order something from the waiter, you don't necessarily need to know how to cook the dish you have ordered. You just place your order. The chef put it on the menu, so that means that the chef knows how to cook it. The chef is your unconscious mind. She knows exactly how to make it happen. If you were able to dream it, it means that your chef knows how to cook it. You would not have been able to imagine it if you did not have what it takes to realize it.

All you have to do is to place your order with the waiter. The waiter will run to the kitchen, and the chef will gather all the ingredients to create your dish. The logical mind is not necessary for this.

When you are clear about what you want and what you expect from your unconscious mind, it starts working for you in the background while you continue to live your life. It guides you into being at the right place at the right time. It whispers answers into your ears when you are about to learn something that will generate results towards your goal. It makes you feel like doing something right. It makes you feel like exercising and eating healthy food. Trust that you have everything you need inside. You got this. Place your order!

The following questions are designed to create a habit for your personal assistant to expect that you will be asking these questions every night. The first few days, it may feel like pulling answers from some James Bond trained spy. Eventually, your unconscious mind will be setting up your day accordingly as it will know that you will be asking for these answers at night and that it better be ready with something to respond to your demand.

PART 3:

YOUR THRIVING GOAL

CHAPTER 3:
ELICIT YOUR
THRIVING GOAL

*You are never too old to set another goal
or to dream a new dream.*

- Les Brown

The first part of the book is to help you elicit your Thriving Goal.

What is the one thing that you want more than anything else? What drives you? What would you defend? What is important to you? If you have read my books from the THINK Yourself® series, you have done this process in the first step of the D.N.A. System. Visualize yourself a year from now. What do you want to have accomplished? How do you want to feel? What kind of people are you attracting to be around you? Who do you want to be? What are you enjoying? What is your life like?

On the next page, you will be invited to write down your goals in a positive statement. You want to state what you want in positive and present terms, i.e. what do you want, where do you want it, and when do you want it? Example: "I am doing or have X".

"My name is.... and I love my new life. I have successfully changed my old behaviours into new habits that are serving me. I can breeze through life in a light way and I have the self-confidence to introduce myself to highly intelligent, healthy and motivated people like me. I am happy to be surrounded by positive influences that keep me on track with my new choices. I always find ways to stay motivated and inspired."

If the statement forms as "I do not want..." then ask yourself: "What do I want instead of..." If you say: "I don't want to be tired anymore, I don't want to be stressed, I don't want to be overweight", it is like asking your contractor to paint your kitchen 'NOT blue'. You have to state what you want, not what you don't want. Use words like energetic, calm, in control, energized, fit, thin, strong.

Avoid all the "...-Free" words like stress-free, alcohol-free, etc. Use the words calm, clean, free, etc.

If it feels totally untrue when you say it out loud, you may want to start your statement with: ''I am willing to learn how it feels..." or "I am in the process of...", giving you permission to evolve.

An example of when the use of a 'progressive' statement of this kind is useful, is when the reverse of what you don't want is totally off-limits. When I work with people going through grief, this becomes very handy. I work with a couple who have lost their daughter. It is terrible. Their life just totally fell apart. Nobody should pass before their parents, it is the reverse of the normal order of things. Devastating.

When we did their thriving goal, they could not say: "I am happy, life is beautiful, etc." They had just lost their baby girl. This statement was totally off-limits. Instead, we structured the sentences this way: "I am willing to learn how it feels to be happy again. I am in the process of learning how to have a beautiful life with my spouse and my son". They also have a son and the love for him will drive them to heal, and with time, feel happiness again.

The same goes for someone who has over 150lbs to lose. They likely cannot look at themselves in the mirror and say: "I am thin and slim, and I feel like I am in the best shape of my life." Again, a progressive statement may be needed here: "I am in the process of reaching my ideal weight." "I am willing to learn how it feels to live an active and healthy lifestyle". "I am in the process of changing my habits to a clean lifestyle".

Here are some examples of outcomes, depending on what you want to focus on.

Business example:

" My name is... and I am feeling great in my office. It is time to meet a very important potential client and I know I am fully prepared and ready. I will wow them and leave the meeting with a signed contract! I got this. I am confident, and I can't wait to tell my family tonight at dinner as I am loving my new schedule of taking the time to enjoy the evening meal every day with them. "

Example of someone whose daughter's wedding is coming up:

"My name is ………. and I am looking great and feeling great in my mother of the bride's dress that I am wearing at my daughter's wedding in July. I am at peace as everything is ready and perfectly planned. I have time to enjoy myself and take full advantage of this perfect day where love is embracing everybody. People are telling me how fabulous I look. I feel proud and

happy to have had the time to be involved in the planning as my successful career allowed me to take the time. I can see my daughter being at her best and tremendously happy. I can smell the scents of the flowers on this gorgeous July day and I have a wonderful feeling going through my body that will keep me happy for years to come."

General example:

"My name is.... and I am in control of my days. I love that I live only a few minutes away from my work and I am really focused and can get a lot done in a single day. Every day when I leave my office, I feel that I have achieved much, and that my work made a difference for someone else. I have time to exercise and eat well and I am in the best shape of my life. I have achieved a work-life balance and my relationship with my significant other is very fulfilling. I always have the time and money to attend un-expected events or to pay expenses for myself or my family, and I always discover what to do and how to be flexible and adapt. I am truly, genuinely happy. I hear people tell me how great I look, and I feel amazing. I love myself."

Your turn, write your positive outcome:

My name is _____ and I ... _____

_____

_____

_____

_____

_____

_____

_____

_____

_____

_____

_____

_____

_____

_____

_____

_____

_____

_____

_____

_____

_____

_____

Once you have written your outcome, place copies of this statement all over your house, in every room and in your car. Write everything as if it's happening in the present, as if it's happening right now.

You can add to your statement as time goes by. It is always good to keep it updated and make sure that your statement changes and evolves with you and your changing desires.

Read this statement several times a day and at least once out loud so that your brain hears it out loud. Keep it at the top of your mind so that your brain will continually remind you of it when times get tough. It will drive you and give you energy to keep going when facing obstacles.

KEEP AT IT

There is a popular belief that it takes 21 days to re-create new neural pathways through the brain, to create the new habit. This idea started in the 1950s, as a result of research conducted by Dr. Maxwell Maltz.[2] He studied patients that were receiving plastic surgery, and discovered that it would take them, on average, 21 days to get used to their new facial features.[3]

As you can realize now, this research, although quite popular, is quite dated. I prefer to follow the results of Dr. Phillippa Lally,[4] who conducted research in 2009 with volunteers who chose a new eating, drinking or activity behaviour to carry out daily, in the same context, for 12 weeks. The study published in the European Journal of Social Psychology reported that the average time to reach automaticity (performing a task without thought) for a new behaviour was 66 days.

Read your positive outcome statement every day for at least 2 months (66 days). If you catch yourself thinking negative thoughts, turn them into positive thoughts. It took years for you to get where you are now, it might take a few months to reset your brain and create new habits.

---

2 Maxwell Maltz, Psycho-Cybernetics, A New Way To Get More Living Out of Life (New York: Prentice-Hall, 1960)
3 http://jamesclear.com/new-habit
4 Phillippa Lally, Dr., "How are habits formed: Modelling habit formation in the real world," European Journal of Social Psychology 40, no. 6, 998-1009

PART 4:

THE

DAILY

QUESTIONS

SECTION 1:
MY "HAVE-DONE LIST"
FOR TODAY

The reward of a thing well done is having done it.
- Ralph Waldo Emerson

A day like many others. Sitting in my office contemplating the piles and piles of different projects I was working on. I had a long to-do list for the day and I knew very well I would more likely only barely touch any item on it as I was usually getting interrupted, distracted, was choosing to procrastinate or was just running out of time.

I had learned a complex system of organizing my schedule which included always ending the day with planning for the next. Every night, I would look at my to-do list and immediately recognize the same feeling of having wasted another day. Feeling like a loser as I had not checked enough boxes. This was not working for me. Although I liked the idea of being organized, I certainly did not like how my endless to-do list was making me feel. I felt like I had failed, although I knew that I was an ambitious person and had actually done many things with the day even if they were not specifically 'on the list'. I could not face another day of feeling this way about my daily accomplishments. I needed a different strategy, and the "Have-Done List" was born.

Unlike a to-do list, the have-done list makes you feel awesome. It gives you energy as you notice what you have done instead of feeling like a failure for what you have not done.

I ACCOMPLISHED THIS TODAY:

This section allows you to take stock of what you have done today. We tend to only look at our to-do list and we sometimes send ourselves negative feelings when we notice we have barely touched whatever was

25

on it. It could be because we wasted time. However, most of the time, it's because something else came up.

With this question, you want to give yourself credit for what you have done.

For example, let's say you had planned to work on an important project all morning. The phone kept ringing and you eventually picked up. A friend was asking you to join them to a networking event. You judged that it would actually be a good idea, considering you had just launched your new business on the side, so you went with your friend. It would be tempting to talk ourselves down at the end of the day for not working on the project you were supposed to. Instead, give yourself credit for doing what you did instead, because it had its own value. Whatever the other thing was, even if it was not on your to-do list, even if you chose to go for coffee with a friend and catch up, that was something. Even if it is as simple as "I went to work".

I TOOK THIS STEP TOWARDS MY GOAL:

This question section is wiring your personal assistant to find something every day that will take you one step closer to your goal. It may be small. Maybe you have simply chosen to go for a walk at lunch time if you have a goal of being fitter. You may have asked a friend to send you the phone number or the web link to register for a class. That is a step. You don't need to have saved a kid from a burning house in order to have something worthy of your have-done list.

SECTION 2:
MY "HAVE-BEEN LIST"
FOR TODAY

Emotions are products of our mind,
and we can actually train ourselves
to choose whether we banish or embrace them.

- Mariella Frostrup

HERE IS A POSITIVE EMOTION
I CHOSE TO FEEL TODAY:

This is making sure your mind is keeping you on your toes. You are in charge of your emotions. When something happens to you, you can step back from being in your head and choose to feel differently. Having to respond to this question daily will trigger your brain to alert you when there is an opportunity for you to choose to be in a specific mood. You will be amazed at how this will transform the way you feel.

For example, you can write something like: "I was driving on my way to work, and I chose to relax and smile at the person that cut me off on the highway. I told myself they were probably in a hurry to drive their pregnant wife to the hospital as her water had just broken". Even if you know it is not true, and that more likely that guy is a moron that obliviously puts everyone's life in danger with his driving style, you ultimately can choose how you respond to it. He certainly doesn't remember you and you more likely did not ruin his day. Why should you let him ruin yours?

**HERE IS A NEW POSITIVE BELIEF
I CHOSE TO CREATE TODAY
OR AN EXISTING POSITIVE BELIEF
THAT SERVED ME TODAY:**

You will become more and more aware of your thoughts. Every time you catch yourself thinking something negative, rephrase it right away. If for example, you hear yourself think: "I am getting so old", you can choose to rephrase it with: "Wait, cancel that. I am actually getting very wise and have lots of experience."

Hear yourself rephrasing your thoughts all day and then choose which ones you want to report to your journal at night. Even if it is the same as the day before.

SECTION 3: GRATITUDES FOR TODAY

Gratitude makes sense of our past,
brings peace for today
and creates a vision for tomorrow
- Melody Beattle

TODAY, I AM GRATEFUL FOR:

This is the best part of your daily gratitude. What are you grateful for?

Let me share with you what keeps me honest. What keeps me from feeling sorry for myself.

I am very blessed that I get to be part of a team that volunteers regularly to help street people find an ear that will listen and respond with a warm caring smile. People in the streets are ignored on a regular basis. They have no home to go to and mostly, they have no-one to turn to. Their stories are all different. They are not bad people. Most of them just ran out of luck. One man lost his young wife to a tragic accident and just could not recover from it. He lost joy and stopped caring. Quit his job and ended up in the streets. A couple lost their child. One young girl works but is barely able to make it with her salary as she only gets part time hours, so she comes to us for her daily dinners as she cannot afford food. The same goes for a family of four who comes to dine with us on a regular basis. Whenever I come back, I always count my blessings and realize how fortunate I am to have people in my life and a home with a warm bed to come to.

What are you grateful for? What are you thankful for today? It can be the same as yesterday. In my journal, it is quite often that the same things come back over and over, and it's okay. And sometimes, it is simply the warm tea I had after coming home on a cold rainy day.

SECTION 4:
MY PLAN
FOR TOMORROW

If you don't design your own life plan,
chances are you'll fall into someone else's plan.
And guess what they have planned for you? Not much.

- Jim Rohn

TOMORROW, I WILL END THE DAY HAVING
DONE THIS IMPORTANT THING:

This question is setting up your day for tomorrow. What is the one thing that is important to you and that you will have done by the end of the day? Plan for it in advance. This tells your personal assistant to make sure to plan time for this the next day. As you write it, have an idea as to when you will address this. Maybe you will start your day with it. Maybe you will carve time in the afternoon to accomplish this task. Know in advance.

You now have everything you need. Start writing your daily gratitude and watch your life transform!

PART 5:

DAILY

GRATITUDE

FORM

DATE: _____

MY "HAVE-DONE-LIST" FOR TODAY
I accomplished this today:

_____

_____

_____

I took this step towards my goal:

_____

_____

_____

MY "HAVE-BEEN-LIST" FOR TODAY
Here is a positive emotion I chose to feel today:

_____

_____

_____

Here is a new positive belief I chose to create today, or, an existing positive belief that served me today:

_____

_____

_____

MY GRATITUDES FOR TODAY
Today, I am grateful for:

_____

_____

_____

MY PLAN FOR TOMORROW
Tomorrow, I will end the day having done this important thing:

_____

_____

DATE: _____

MY "HAVE-DONE-LIST" FOR TODAY
I accomplished this today:

_____

_____

_____

I took this step towards my goal:

_____

_____

_____

MY "HAVE-BEEN-LIST" FOR TODAY
Here is a positive emotion I chose to feel today:

_____

_____

_____

Here is a new positive belief I chose to create today, or, an existing positive belief that served me today:

_____

_____

_____

MY GRATITUDES FOR TODAY
Today, I am grateful for:

_____

_____

_____

MY PLAN FOR TOMORROW
Tomorrow, I will end the day having done this important thing:

_____

_____

DATE: _____

MY "HAVE-DONE-LIST" FOR TODAY
I accomplished this today:

_____

_____

_____

I took this step towards my goal:

_____

_____

_____

MY "HAVE-BEEN-LIST" FOR TODAY
Here is a positive emotion I chose to feel today:

_____

_____

_____

Here is a new positive belief I chose to create today, or, an existing positive belief that served me today:

_____

_____

_____

MY GRATITUDES FOR TODAY
Today, I am grateful for:

_____

_____

_____

MY PLAN FOR TOMORROW
Tomorrow, I will end the day having done this important thing:

_____

_____

DATE: _____

MY "HAVE-DONE-LIST" FOR TODAY
I accomplished this today:

_____

_____

_____

I took this step towards my goal:

_____

_____

_____

MY "HAVE-BEEN-LIST" FOR TODAY
Here is a positive emotion I chose to feel today:

_____

_____

_____

Here is a new positive belief I chose to create today, or, an existing positive belief that served me today:

_____

_____

_____

MY GRATITUDES FOR TODAY
Today, I am grateful for:

_____

_____

_____

MY PLAN FOR TOMORROW
Tomorrow, I will end the day having done this important thing:

_____

_____

DATE: _____

MY "HAVE-DONE-LIST" FOR TODAY
I accomplished this today:

_____

_____

_____

I took this step towards my goal:

_____

_____

_____

MY "HAVE-BEEN-LIST" FOR TODAY
Here is a positive emotion I chose to feel today:

_____

_____

_____

Here is a new positive belief I chose to create today, or, an existing positive belief that served me today:

_____

_____

_____

MY GRATITUDES FOR TODAY
Today, I am grateful for:

_____

_____

_____

MY PLAN FOR TOMORROW
Tomorrow, I will end the day having done this important thing:

_____

_____

DATE: _____

MY "HAVE-DONE-LIST" FOR TODAY
I accomplished this today:

_____

_____

_____

I took this step towards my goal:

_____

_____

_____

MY "HAVE-BEEN-LIST" FOR TODAY
Here is a positive emotion I chose to feel today:

_____

_____

_____

Here is a new positive belief I chose to create today, or, an existing positive belief that served me today:

_____

_____

_____

MY GRATITUDES FOR TODAY
Today, I am grateful for:

_____

_____

_____

MY PLAN FOR TOMORROW
Tomorrow, I will end the day having done this important thing:

_____

_____

DATE: _____

MY "HAVE-DONE-LIST" FOR TODAY
I accomplished this today:

_____

_____

_____

I took this step towards my goal:

_____

_____

_____

MY "HAVE-BEEN-LIST" FOR TODAY
Here is a positive emotion I chose to feel today:

_____

_____

_____

Here is a new positive belief I chose to create today, or, an existing positive belief that served me today:

_____

_____

_____

MY GRATITUDES FOR TODAY
Today, I am grateful for:

_____

_____

_____

MY PLAN FOR TOMORROW
Tomorrow, I will end the day having done this important thing:

_____

_____

DATE: _____

MY "HAVE-DONE-LIST" FOR TODAY
I accomplished this today:

_____

_____

_____

I took this step towards my goal:

_____

_____

_____

MY "HAVE-BEEN-LIST" FOR TODAY
Here is a positive emotion I chose to feel today:

_____

_____

_____

Here is a new positive belief I chose to create today, or, an existing positive belief that served me today:

_____

_____

_____

MY GRATITUDES FOR TODAY
Today, I am grateful for:

_____

_____

_____

MY PLAN FOR TOMORROW
Tomorrow, I will end the day having done this important thing:

_____

_____

DATE: _____

MY "HAVE-DONE-LIST" FOR TODAY
I accomplished this today:

_____

_____

_____

I took this step towards my goal:

_____

_____

_____

MY "HAVE-BEEN-LIST" FOR TODAY
Here is a positive emotion I chose to feel today:

_____

_____

Here is a new positive belief I chose to create today, or, an existing positive belief that served me today:

_____

_____

_____

MY GRATITUDES FOR TODAY
Today, I am grateful for:

_____

_____

MY PLAN FOR TOMORROW
Tomorrow, I will end the day having done this important thing:

_____

_____

DATE: _____

MY "HAVE-DONE-LIST" FOR TODAY
I accomplished this today:

_____

_____

_____

I took this step towards my goal:

_____

_____

_____

MY "HAVE-BEEN-LIST" FOR TODAY
Here is a positive emotion I chose to feel today:

_____

_____

_____

Here is a new positive belief I chose to create today, or, an existing positive belief that served me today:

_____

_____

_____

MY GRATITUDES FOR TODAY
Today, I am grateful for:

_____

_____

_____

MY PLAN FOR TOMORROW
Tomorrow, I will end the day having done this important thing:

_____

_____

DATE: _____

MY "HAVE-DONE-LIST" FOR TODAY
I accomplished this today:

_____

_____

_____

I took this step towards my goal:

_____

_____

_____

MY "HAVE-BEEN-LIST" FOR TODAY
Here is a positive emotion I chose to feel today:

_____

_____

_____

Here is a new positive belief I chose to create today, or, an existing positive belief that served me today:

_____

_____

_____

MY GRATITUDES FOR TODAY
Today, I am grateful for:

_____

_____

_____

MY PLAN FOR TOMORROW
Tomorrow, I will end the day having done this important thing:

_____

_____

DATE: _____

MY "HAVE-DONE-LIST" FOR TODAY
I accomplished this today:

_____

_____

_____

I took this step towards my goal:

_____

_____

_____

MY "HAVE-BEEN-LIST" FOR TODAY
Here is a positive emotion I chose to feel today:

_____

_____

_____

Here is a new positive belief I chose to create today, or, an existing positive belief that served me today:

_____

_____

_____

MY GRATITUDES FOR TODAY
Today, I am grateful for:

_____

_____

_____

MY PLAN FOR TOMORROW
Tomorrow, I will end the day having done this important thing:

_____

_____

DATE: _____

MY "HAVE-DONE-LIST" FOR TODAY
I accomplished this today:

_____

_____

_____

I took this step towards my goal:

_____

_____

_____

MY "HAVE-BEEN-LIST" FOR TODAY
Here is a positive emotion I chose to feel today:

_____

_____

_____

Here is a new positive belief I chose to create today, or, an existing positive belief that served me today:

_____

_____

_____

MY GRATITUDES FOR TODAY
Today, I am grateful for:

_____

_____

_____

MY PLAN FOR TOMORROW
Tomorrow, I will end the day having done this important thing:

_____

_____

DATE: _____

MY "HAVE-DONE-LIST" FOR TODAY
I accomplished this today:

_____

_____

_____

I took this step towards my goal:

_____

_____

_____

MY "HAVE-BEEN-LIST" FOR TODAY
Here is a positive emotion I chose to feel today:

_____

_____

_____

Here is a new positive belief I chose to create today, or, an existing positive belief that served me today:

_____

_____

_____

MY GRATITUDES FOR TODAY
Today, I am grateful for:

_____

_____

_____

MY PLAN FOR TOMORROW
Tomorrow, I will end the day having done this important thing:

_____

_____

DATE: _____

MY "HAVE-DONE-LIST" FOR TODAY
I accomplished this today:

_____

_____

_____

I took this step towards my goal:

_____

_____

_____

MY "HAVE-BEEN-LIST" FOR TODAY
Here is a positive emotion I chose to feel today:

_____

_____

_____

Here is a new positive belief I chose to create today, or, an existing positive belief that served me today:

_____

_____

_____

MY GRATITUDES FOR TODAY
Today, I am grateful for:

_____

_____

_____

MY PLAN FOR TOMORROW
Tomorrow, I will end the day having done this important thing:

_____

_____

DATE: _____

MY "HAVE-DONE-LIST" FOR TODAY
I accomplished this today:

_____

_____

_____

I took this step towards my goal:

_____

_____

_____

MY "HAVE-BEEN-LIST" FOR TODAY
Here is a positive emotion I chose to feel today:

_____

_____

_____

Here is a new positive belief I chose to create today, or, an existing positive belief that served me today:

_____

_____

_____

MY GRATITUDES FOR TODAY
Today, I am grateful for:

_____

_____

_____

MY PLAN FOR TOMORROW
Tomorrow, I will end the day having done this important thing:

_____

_____

DATE: _____

MY "HAVE-DONE-LIST" FOR TODAY
I accomplished this today:

_____

_____

_____

I took this step towards my goal:

_____

_____

_____

MY "HAVE-BEEN-LIST" FOR TODAY
Here is a positive emotion I chose to feel today:

_____

_____

_____

Here is a new positive belief I chose to create today, or, an existing positive belief that served me today:

_____

_____

_____

MY GRATITUDES FOR TODAY
Today, I am grateful for:

_____

_____

_____

MY PLAN FOR TOMORROW
Tomorrow, I will end the day having done this important thing:

_____

_____

DATE: _____

MY "HAVE-DONE-LIST" FOR TODAY
I accomplished this today:

_____

_____

_____

I took this step towards my goal:

_____

_____

_____

MY "HAVE-BEEN-LIST" FOR TODAY
Here is a positive emotion I chose to feel today:

_____

_____

_____

Here is a new positive belief I chose to create today, or, an existing positive belief that served me today:

_____

_____

_____

MY GRATITUDES FOR TODAY
Today, I am grateful for:

_____

_____

_____

MY PLAN FOR TOMORROW
Tomorrow, I will end the day having done this important thing:

_____

_____

DATE: _____

MY "HAVE-DONE-LIST" FOR TODAY
I accomplished this today:

_____

_____

_____

I took this step towards my goal:

_____

_____

_____

MY "HAVE-BEEN-LIST" FOR TODAY
Here is a positive emotion I chose to feel today:

_____

_____

_____

Here is a new positive belief I chose to create today, or, an existing positive belief that served me today:

_____

_____

_____

MY GRATITUDES FOR TODAY
Today, I am grateful for:

_____

_____

_____

MY PLAN FOR TOMORROW
Tomorrow, I will end the day having done this important thing:

_____

_____

DATE: _____

MY "HAVE-DONE-LIST" FOR TODAY
I accomplished this today:

_____

_____

_____

I took this step towards my goal:

_____

_____

_____

MY "HAVE-BEEN-LIST" FOR TODAY
Here is a positive emotion I chose to feel today:

_____

_____

_____

Here is a new positive belief I chose to create today, or, an existing positive belief that served me today:

_____

_____

_____

MY GRATITUDES FOR TODAY
Today, I am grateful for:

_____

_____

_____

MY PLAN FOR TOMORROW
Tomorrow, I will end the day having done this important thing:

_____

_____

DATE: _____

MY "HAVE-DONE-LIST" FOR TODAY
I accomplished this today:

_____

_____

_____

I took this step towards my goal:

_____

_____

_____

MY "HAVE-BEEN-LIST" FOR TODAY
Here is a positive emotion I chose to feel today:

_____

_____

_____

Here is a new positive belief I chose to create today, or, an existing positive belief that served me today:

_____

_____

_____

MY GRATITUDES FOR TODAY
Today, I am grateful for:

_____

_____

_____

MY PLAN FOR TOMORROW
Tomorrow, I will end the day having done this important thing:

_____

_____

DATE: _____

MY "HAVE-DONE-LIST" FOR TODAY
I accomplished this today:

_____

_____

_____

I took this step towards my goal:

_____

_____

_____

MY "HAVE-BEEN-LIST" FOR TODAY
Here is a positive emotion I chose to feel today:

_____

_____

_____

Here is a new positive belief I chose to create today, or, an existing positive belief that served me today:

_____

_____

_____

MY GRATITUDES FOR TODAY
Today, I am grateful for:

_____

_____

_____

MY PLAN FOR TOMORROW
Tomorrow, I will end the day having done this important thing:

_____

_____

DATE: _____

MY "HAVE-DONE-LIST" FOR TODAY
I accomplished this today:

_____

_____

_____

I took this step towards my goal:

_____

_____

_____

MY "HAVE-BEEN-LIST" FOR TODAY
Here is a positive emotion I chose to feel today:

_____

_____

_____

Here is a new positive belief I chose to create today, or, an existing positive belief that served me today:

_____

_____

_____

MY GRATITUDES FOR TODAY
Today, I am grateful for:

_____

_____

_____

MY PLAN FOR TOMORROW
Tomorrow, I will end the day having done this important thing:

_____

_____

DATE: _____

MY "HAVE-DONE-LIST" FOR TODAY
I accomplished this today:

_____

_____

_____

I took this step towards my goal:

_____

_____

_____

MY "HAVE-BEEN-LIST" FOR TODAY
Here is a positive emotion I chose to feel today:

_____

_____

_____

Here is a new positive belief I chose to create today, or, an existing positive belief that served me today:

_____

_____

_____

MY GRATITUDES FOR TODAY
Today, I am grateful for:

_____

_____

_____

MY PLAN FOR TOMORROW
Tomorrow, I will end the day having done this important thing:

_____

_____

MY "HAVE-DONE-LIST" FOR TODAY
I accomplished this today:

_____

_____

_____

I took this step towards my goal:

_____

_____

_____

MY "HAVE-BEEN-LIST" FOR TODAY
Here is a positive emotion I chose to feel today:

_____

_____

_____

Here is a new positive belief I chose to create today, or, an existing positive belief that served me today:

_____

_____

_____

MY GRATITUDES FOR TODAY
Today, I am grateful for:

_____

_____

_____

MY PLAN FOR TOMORROW
Tomorrow, I will end the day having done this important thing:

_____

_____

DATE: _____

MY "HAVE-DONE-LIST" FOR TODAY
I accomplished this today:

_____

_____

_____

I took this step towards my goal:

_____

_____

_____

MY "HAVE-BEEN-LIST" FOR TODAY
Here is a positive emotion I chose to feel today:

_____

_____

_____

Here is a new positive belief I chose to create today, or, an existing positive belief that served me today:

_____

_____

_____

MY GRATITUDES FOR TODAY
Today, I am grateful for:

_____

_____

_____

MY PLAN FOR TOMORROW
Tomorrow, I will end the day having done this important thing:

_____

_____

MY "HAVE-DONE-LIST" FOR TODAY
I accomplished this today:

_____

_____

_____

I took this step towards my goal:

_____

_____

_____

MY "HAVE-BEEN-LIST" FOR TODAY
Here is a positive emotion I chose to feel today:

_____

_____

_____

Here is a new positive belief I chose to create today, or, an existing positive belief that served me today:

_____

_____

_____

MY GRATITUDES FOR TODAY
Today, I am grateful for:

_____

_____

_____

MY PLAN FOR TOMORROW
Tomorrow, I will end the day having done this important thing:

_____

_____

DATE: _____

MY "HAVE-DONE-LIST" FOR TODAY
I accomplished this today:

_____

_____

_____

I took this step towards my goal:

_____

_____

_____

MY "HAVE-BEEN-LIST" FOR TODAY
Here is a positive emotion I chose to feel today:

_____

_____

_____

Here is a new positive belief I chose to create today, or, an existing positive belief that served me today:

_____

_____

_____

MY GRATITUDES FOR TODAY
Today, I am grateful for:

_____

_____

_____

MY PLAN FOR TOMORROW
Tomorrow, I will end the day having done this important thing:

_____

_____

DATE: _____

MY "HAVE-DONE-LIST" FOR TODAY
I accomplished this today:

_____

_____

_____

I took this step towards my goal:

_____

_____

_____

MY "HAVE-BEEN-LIST" FOR TODAY
Here is a positive emotion I chose to feel today:

_____

_____

_____

Here is a new positive belief I chose to create today, or, an existing positive belief that served me today:

_____

_____

_____

MY GRATITUDES FOR TODAY
Today, I am grateful for:

_____

_____

_____

MY PLAN FOR TOMORROW
Tomorrow, I will end the day having done this important thing:

_____

_____

DATE: _____

MY "HAVE-DONE-LIST" FOR TODAY
I accomplished this today:

_____

_____

_____

I took this step towards my goal:

_____

_____

_____

MY "HAVE-BEEN-LIST" FOR TODAY
Here is a positive emotion I chose to feel today:

_____

_____

_____

Here is a new positive belief I chose to create today, or, an existing positive belief that served me today:

_____

_____

_____

MY GRATITUDES FOR TODAY
Today, I am grateful for:

_____

_____

_____

MY PLAN FOR TOMORROW
Tomorrow, I will end the day having done this important thing:

_____

_____

DATE: _____

MY "HAVE-DONE-LIST" FOR TODAY
I accomplished this today:

_____

_____

_____

I took this step towards my goal:

_____

_____

_____

MY "HAVE-BEEN-LIST" FOR TODAY
Here is a positive emotion I chose to feel today:

_____

_____

_____

Here is a new positive belief I chose to create today, or, an existing positive belief that served me today:

_____

_____

_____

MY GRATITUDES FOR TODAY
Today, I am grateful for:

_____

_____

_____

MY PLAN FOR TOMORROW
Tomorrow, I will end the day having done this important thing:

_____

_____

DATE: _____

MY "HAVE-DONE-LIST" FOR TODAY
I accomplished this today:

_____

_____

_____

I took this step towards my goal:

_____

_____

_____

MY "HAVE-BEEN-LIST" FOR TODAY
Here is a positive emotion I chose to feel today:

_____

_____

_____

Here is a new positive belief I chose to create today, or, an existing positive belief that served me today:

_____

_____

_____

MY GRATITUDES FOR TODAY
Today, I am grateful for:

_____

_____

_____

MY PLAN FOR TOMORROW
Tomorrow, I will end the day having done this important thing:

_____

_____

DATE: _____

MY "HAVE-DONE-LIST" FOR TODAY
I accomplished this today:

_____

_____

_____

I took this step towards my goal:

_____

_____

_____

MY "HAVE-BEEN-LIST" FOR TODAY
Here is a positive emotion I chose to feel today:

_____

_____

_____

Here is a new positive belief I chose to create today, or, an existing positive belief that served me today:

_____

_____

_____

MY GRATITUDES FOR TODAY
Today, I am grateful for:

_____

_____

_____

MY PLAN FOR TOMORROW
Tomorrow, I will end the day having done this important thing:

_____

_____

DATE: _____

MY "HAVE-DONE-LIST" FOR TODAY
I accomplished this today:

_____

_____

_____

I took this step towards my goal:

_____

_____

_____

MY "HAVE-BEEN-LIST" FOR TODAY
Here is a positive emotion I chose to feel today:

_____

_____

_____

Here is a new positive belief I chose to create today, or, an existing positive belief that served me today:

_____

_____

_____

MY GRATITUDES FOR TODAY
Today, I am grateful for:

_____

_____

_____

MY PLAN FOR TOMORROW
Tomorrow, I will end the day having done this important thing:

_____

_____

DATE: _____

MY "HAVE-DONE-LIST" FOR TODAY
I accomplished this today:

_____

_____

_____

I took this step towards my goal:

_____

_____

_____

MY "HAVE-BEEN-LIST" FOR TODAY
Here is a positive emotion I chose to feel today:

_____

_____

_____

Here is a new positive belief I chose to create today, or, an existing positive belief that served me today:

_____

_____

_____

MY GRATITUDES FOR TODAY
Today, I am grateful for:

_____

_____

_____

MY PLAN FOR TOMORROW
Tomorrow, I will end the day having done this important thing:

_____

_____

DATE: _____

MY "HAVE-DONE-LIST" FOR TODAY
I accomplished this today:

_____

_____

_____

I took this step towards my goal:

_____

_____

_____

MY "HAVE-BEEN-LIST" FOR TODAY
Here is a positive emotion I chose to feel today:

_____

_____

_____

Here is a new positive belief I chose to create today, or, an existing positive belief that served me today:

_____

_____

_____

MY GRATITUDES FOR TODAY
Today, I am grateful for:

_____

_____

_____

MY PLAN FOR TOMORROW
Tomorrow, I will end the day having done this important thing:

_____

_____

MY "HAVE-DONE-LIST" FOR TODAY
I accomplished this today:

_____

_____

_____

I took this step towards my goal:

_____

_____

_____

MY "HAVE-BEEN-LIST" FOR TODAY
Here is a positive emotion I chose to feel today:

_____

_____

_____

Here is a new positive belief I chose to create today, or, an existing positive belief that served me today:

_____

_____

_____

MY GRATITUDES FOR TODAY
Today, I am grateful for:

_____

_____

_____

MY PLAN FOR TOMORROW
Tomorrow, I will end the day having done this important thing:

_____

_____

DATE: _____

MY "HAVE-DONE-LIST" FOR TODAY
I accomplished this today:

_____

_____

_____

I took this step towards my goal:

_____

_____

_____

MY "HAVE-BEEN-LIST" FOR TODAY
Here is a positive emotion I chose to feel today:

_____

_____

_____

Here is a new positive belief I chose to create today, or, an existing positive belief that served me today:

_____

_____

_____

MY GRATITUDES FOR TODAY
Today, I am grateful for:

_____

_____

_____

MY PLAN FOR TOMORROW
Tomorrow, I will end the day having done this important thing:

_____

_____

DATE: _____

MY "HAVE-DONE-LIST" FOR TODAY
I accomplished this today:

_____

_____

_____

I took this step towards my goal:

_____

_____

_____

MY "HAVE-BEEN-LIST" FOR TODAY
Here is a positive emotion I chose to feel today:

_____

_____

_____

Here is a new positive belief I chose to create today, or, an existing positive belief that served me today:

_____

_____

_____

MY GRATITUDES FOR TODAY
Today, I am grateful for:

_____

_____

_____

MY PLAN FOR TOMORROW
Tomorrow, I will end the day having done this important thing:

_____

_____

DATE: _____

MY "HAVE-DONE-LIST" FOR TODAY
I accomplished this today:

_____

_____

_____

I took this step towards my goal:

_____

_____

_____

MY "HAVE-BEEN-LIST" FOR TODAY
Here is a positive emotion I chose to feel today:

_____

_____

_____

Here is a new positive belief I chose to create today, or, an existing positive belief that served me today:

_____

_____

_____

MY GRATITUDES FOR TODAY
Today, I am grateful for:

_____

_____

_____

MY PLAN FOR TOMORROW
Tomorrow, I will end the day having done this important thing:

_____

_____

DATE: _____

MY "HAVE-DONE-LIST" FOR TODAY
I accomplished this today:

_____

_____

_____

I took this step towards my goal:

_____

_____

_____

MY "HAVE-BEEN-LIST" FOR TODAY
Here is a positive emotion I chose to feel today:

_____

_____

_____

Here is a new positive belief I chose to create today, or, an existing positive belief that served me today:

_____

_____

_____

MY GRATITUDES FOR TODAY
Today, I am grateful for:

_____

_____

_____

MY PLAN FOR TOMORROW
Tomorrow, I will end the day having done this important thing:

_____

_____

DATE: _____

MY "HAVE-DONE-LIST" FOR TODAY
I accomplished this today:

_____

_____

_____

I took this step towards my goal:

_____

_____

_____

MY "HAVE-BEEN-LIST" FOR TODAY
Here is a positive emotion I chose to feel today:

_____

_____

_____

Here is a new positive belief I chose to create today, or, an existing positive belief that served me today:

_____

_____

_____

MY GRATITUDES FOR TODAY
Today, I am grateful for:

_____

_____

_____

MY PLAN FOR TOMORROW
Tomorrow, I will end the day having done this important thing:

_____

_____

DATE: _____

MY "HAVE-DONE-LIST" FOR TODAY
I accomplished this today:

_____

_____

_____

I took this step towards my goal:

_____

_____

_____

MY "HAVE-BEEN-LIST" FOR TODAY
Here is a positive emotion I chose to feel today:

_____

_____

_____

Here is a new positive belief I chose to create today, or, an existing positive belief that served me today:

_____

_____

_____

MY GRATITUDES FOR TODAY
Today, I am grateful for:

_____

_____

_____

MY PLAN FOR TOMORROW
Tomorrow, I will end the day having done this important thing:

_____

_____

DATE: _____

MY "HAVE-DONE-LIST" FOR TODAY
I accomplished this today:

_____

_____

_____

I took this step towards my goal:

_____

_____

_____

MY "HAVE-BEEN-LIST" FOR TODAY
Here is a positive emotion I chose to feel today:

_____

_____

Here is a new positive belief I chose to create today, or, an existing positive belief that served me today:

_____

_____

_____

MY GRATITUDES FOR TODAY
Today, I am grateful for:

_____

_____

MY PLAN FOR TOMORROW
Tomorrow, I will end the day having done this important thing:

_____

_____

DATE: _____

MY "HAVE-DONE-LIST" FOR TODAY
I accomplished this today:

_____

_____

_____

I took this step towards my goal:

_____

_____

_____

MY "HAVE-BEEN-LIST" FOR TODAY
Here is a positive emotion I chose to feel today:

_____

_____

_____

Here is a new positive belief I chose to create today, or, an existing positive belief that served me today:

_____

_____

_____

MY GRATITUDES FOR TODAY
Today, I am grateful for:

_____

_____

_____

MY PLAN FOR TOMORROW
Tomorrow, I will end the day having done this important thing:

_____

_____

DATE: _____

MY "HAVE-DONE-LIST" FOR TODAY
I accomplished this today:

_____

_____

_____

I took this step towards my goal:

_____

_____

_____

MY "HAVE-BEEN-LIST" FOR TODAY
Here is a positive emotion I chose to feel today:

_____

_____

_____

Here is a new positive belief I chose to create today, or, an existing positive belief that served me today:

_____

_____

_____

MY GRATITUDES FOR TODAY
Today, I am grateful for:

_____

_____

_____

MY PLAN FOR TOMORROW
Tomorrow, I will end the day having done this important thing:

_____

_____

DATE: _____

MY "HAVE-DONE-LIST" FOR TODAY
I accomplished this today:

_____

_____

_____

I took this step towards my goal:

_____

_____

_____

MY "HAVE-BEEN-LIST" FOR TODAY
Here is a positive emotion I chose to feel today:

_____

_____

_____

Here is a new positive belief I chose to create today, or, an existing positive belief that served me today:

_____

_____

_____

MY GRATITUDES FOR TODAY
Today, I am grateful for:

_____

_____

_____

MY PLAN FOR TOMORROW
Tomorrow, I will end the day having done this important thing:

_____

_____

DATE: _____

MY "HAVE-DONE-LIST" FOR TODAY
I accomplished this today:

_____

_____

_____

I took this step towards my goal:

_____

_____

_____

MY "HAVE-BEEN-LIST" FOR TODAY
Here is a positive emotion I chose to feel today:

_____

_____

_____

Here is a new positive belief I chose to create today, or, an existing positive belief that served me today:

_____

_____

_____

MY GRATITUDES FOR TODAY
Today, I am grateful for:

_____

_____

_____

MY PLAN FOR TOMORROW
Tomorrow, I will end the day having done this important thing:

_____

_____

DATE: _____

MY "HAVE-DONE-LIST" FOR TODAY
I accomplished this today:

_____

_____

_____

I took this step towards my goal:

_____

_____

_____

MY "HAVE-BEEN-LIST" FOR TODAY
Here is a positive emotion I chose to feel today:

_____

_____

_____

Here is a new positive belief I chose to create today, or, an existing positive belief that served me today:

_____

_____

_____

MY GRATITUDES FOR TODAY
Today, I am grateful for:

_____

_____

_____

MY PLAN FOR TOMORROW
Tomorrow, I will end the day having done this important thing:

_____

_____

DATE: _____

MY "HAVE-DONE-LIST" FOR TODAY
I accomplished this today:

_____

_____

_____

I took this step towards my goal:

_____

_____

_____

MY "HAVE-BEEN-LIST" FOR TODAY
Here is a positive emotion I chose to feel today:

_____

_____

_____

Here is a new positive belief I chose to create today, or, an existing positive belief that served me today:

_____

_____

_____

MY GRATITUDES FOR TODAY
Today, I am grateful for:

_____

_____

_____

MY PLAN FOR TOMORROW
Tomorrow, I will end the day having done this important thing:

_____

_____

DATE: _____

MY "HAVE-DONE-LIST" FOR TODAY
I accomplished this today:

_____

_____

_____

I took this step towards my goal:

_____

_____

_____

MY "HAVE-BEEN-LIST" FOR TODAY
Here is a positive emotion I chose to feel today:

_____

_____

_____

Here is a new positive belief I chose to create today, or, an existing positive belief that served me today:

_____

_____

_____

MY GRATITUDES FOR TODAY
Today, I am grateful for:

_____

_____

_____

MY PLAN FOR TOMORROW
Tomorrow, I will end the day having done this important thing:

_____

_____

DATE: _____

MY "HAVE-DONE-LIST" FOR TODAY
I accomplished this today:

_____

_____

_____

I took this step towards my goal:

_____

_____

_____

MY "HAVE-BEEN-LIST" FOR TODAY
Here is a positive emotion I chose to feel today:

_____

_____

_____

Here is a new positive belief I chose to create today, or, an existing positive belief that served me today:

_____

_____

_____

MY GRATITUDES FOR TODAY
Today, I am grateful for:

_____

_____

_____

MY PLAN FOR TOMORROW
Tomorrow, I will end the day having done this important thing:

_____

_____

DATE: _____

MY "HAVE-DONE-LIST" FOR TODAY
I accomplished this today:

_____

_____

_____

I took this step towards my goal:

_____

_____

_____

MY "HAVE-BEEN-LIST" FOR TODAY
Here is a positive emotion I chose to feel today:

_____

_____

_____

Here is a new positive belief I chose to create today, or, an existing positive belief that served me today:

_____

_____

_____

MY GRATITUDES FOR TODAY
Today, I am grateful for:

_____

_____

_____

MY PLAN FOR TOMORROW
Tomorrow, I will end the day having done this important thing:

_____

_____

DATE: _____

MY "HAVE-DONE-LIST" FOR TODAY
I accomplished this today:

_____

_____

_____

I took this step towards my goal:

_____

_____

_____

MY "HAVE-BEEN-LIST" FOR TODAY
Here is a positive emotion I chose to feel today:

_____

_____

_____

Here is a new positive belief I chose to create today, or, an existing positive belief that served me today:

_____

_____

_____

MY GRATITUDES FOR TODAY
Today, I am grateful for:

_____

_____

_____

MY PLAN FOR TOMORROW
Tomorrow, I will end the day having done this important thing:

_____

_____

DATE: _____

MY "HAVE-DONE-LIST" FOR TODAY
I accomplished this today:

_____

_____

_____

I took this step towards my goal:

_____

_____

_____

MY "HAVE-BEEN-LIST" FOR TODAY
Here is a positive emotion I chose to feel today:

_____

_____

_____

Here is a new positive belief I chose to create today, or, an existing positive belief that served me today:

_____

_____

_____

MY GRATITUDES FOR TODAY
Today, I am grateful for:

_____

_____

_____

MY PLAN FOR TOMORROW
Tomorrow, I will end the day having done this important thing:

_____

_____

DATE: _____

MY "HAVE-DONE-LIST" FOR TODAY
I accomplished this today:

_____

_____

_____

I took this step towards my goal:

_____

_____

_____

MY "HAVE-BEEN-LIST" FOR TODAY
Here is a positive emotion I chose to feel today:

_____

_____

_____

Here is a new positive belief I chose to create today, or, an existing positive belief that served me today:

_____

_____

_____

MY GRATITUDES FOR TODAY
Today, I am grateful for:

_____

_____

_____

MY PLAN FOR TOMORROW
Tomorrow, I will end the day having done this important thing:

_____

_____

DATE: _____

MY "HAVE-DONE-LIST" FOR TODAY
I accomplished this today:

_____

_____

_____

I took this step towards my goal:

_____

_____

_____

MY "HAVE-BEEN-LIST" FOR TODAY
Here is a positive emotion I chose to feel today:

_____

_____

_____

Here is a new positive belief I chose to create today, or, an existing positive belief that served me today:

_____

_____

_____

MY GRATITUDES FOR TODAY
Today, I am grateful for:

_____

_____

_____

MY PLAN FOR TOMORROW
Tomorrow, I will end the day having done this important thing:

_____

_____

DATE: _____

MY "HAVE-DONE-LIST" FOR TODAY
I accomplished this today:

_____

_____

_____

I took this step towards my goal:

_____

_____

_____

MY "HAVE-BEEN-LIST" FOR TODAY
Here is a positive emotion I chose to feel today:

_____

_____

_____

Here is a new positive belief I chose to create today, or, an existing positive belief that served me today:

_____

_____

_____

MY GRATITUDES FOR TODAY
Today, I am grateful for:

_____

_____

_____

MY PLAN FOR TOMORROW
Tomorrow, I will end the day having done this important thing:

_____

_____

DATE: _____

MY "HAVE-DONE-LIST" FOR TODAY
I accomplished this today:

_____

_____

_____

I took this step towards my goal:

_____

_____

_____

MY "HAVE-BEEN-LIST" FOR TODAY
Here is a positive emotion I chose to feel today:

_____

_____

_____

Here is a new positive belief I chose to create today, or, an existing positive belief that served me today:

_____

_____

_____

MY GRATITUDES FOR TODAY
Today, I am grateful for:

_____

_____

_____

MY PLAN FOR TOMORROW
Tomorrow, I will end the day having done this important thing:

_____

_____

DATE: _____

MY "HAVE-DONE-LIST" FOR TODAY
I accomplished this today:

_____

_____

_____

I took this step towards my goal:

_____

_____

_____

MY "HAVE-BEEN-LIST" FOR TODAY
Here is a positive emotion I chose to feel today:

_____

_____

_____

Here is a new positive belief I chose to create today, or, an existing positive belief that served me today:

_____

_____

_____

MY GRATITUDES FOR TODAY
Today, I am grateful for:

_____

_____

_____

MY PLAN FOR TOMORROW
Tomorrow, I will end the day having done this important thing:

_____

_____

DATE: _____

MY "HAVE-DONE-LIST" FOR TODAY
I accomplished this today:

_____

_____

_____

I took this step towards my goal:

_____

_____

_____

MY "HAVE-BEEN-LIST" FOR TODAY
Here is a positive emotion I chose to feel today:

_____

_____

_____

Here is a new positive belief I chose to create today, or, an existing positive belief that served me today:

_____

_____

_____

MY GRATITUDES FOR TODAY
Today, I am grateful for:

_____

_____

_____

MY PLAN FOR TOMORROW
Tomorrow, I will end the day having done this important thing:

_____

_____

DATE: _____

MY "HAVE-DONE-LIST" FOR TODAY
I accomplished this today:

_____

_____

_____

I took this step towards my goal:

_____

_____

_____

MY "HAVE-BEEN-LIST" FOR TODAY
Here is a positive emotion I chose to feel today:

_____

_____

_____

Here is a new positive belief I chose to create today, or, an existing positive belief that served me today:

_____

_____

_____

MY GRATITUDES FOR TODAY
Today, I am grateful for:

_____

_____

_____

MY PLAN FOR TOMORROW
Tomorrow, I will end the day having done this important thing:

_____

_____

DATE: _____

MY "HAVE-DONE-LIST" FOR TODAY
I accomplished this today:

_____

_____

_____

I took this step towards my goal:

_____

_____

_____

MY "HAVE-BEEN-LIST" FOR TODAY
Here is a positive emotion I chose to feel today:

_____

_____

_____

Here is a new positive belief I chose to create today, or, an existing positive belief that served me today:

_____

_____

_____

MY GRATITUDES FOR TODAY
Today, I am grateful for:

_____

_____

_____

MY PLAN FOR TOMORROW
Tomorrow, I will end the day having done this important thing:

_____

_____

DATE: _____

MY "HAVE-DONE-LIST" FOR TODAY
I accomplished this today:

_____

_____

_____

I took this step towards my goal:

_____

_____

_____

MY "HAVE-BEEN-LIST" FOR TODAY
Here is a positive emotion I chose to feel today:

_____

_____

_____

Here is a new positive belief I chose to create today, or, an existing positive belief that served me today:

_____

_____

_____

MY GRATITUDES FOR TODAY
Today, I am grateful for:

_____

_____

_____

MY PLAN FOR TOMORROW
Tomorrow, I will end the day having done this important thing:

_____

_____

DATE: _____

MY "HAVE-DONE-LIST" FOR TODAY
I accomplished this today:

_____

_____

_____

I took this step towards my goal:

_____

_____

_____

MY "HAVE-BEEN-LIST" FOR TODAY
Here is a positive emotion I chose to feel today:

_____

_____

_____

Here is a new positive belief I chose to create today, or, an existing positive belief that served me today:

_____

_____

_____

MY GRATITUDES FOR TODAY
Today, I am grateful for:

_____

_____

_____

MY PLAN FOR TOMORROW
Tomorrow, I will end the day having done this important thing:

_____

_____

DATE: _____

MY "HAVE-DONE-LIST" FOR TODAY
I accomplished this today:

_____

_____

_____

I took this step towards my goal:

_____

_____

_____

MY "HAVE-BEEN-LIST" FOR TODAY
Here is a positive emotion I chose to feel today:

_____

_____

_____

Here is a new positive belief I chose to create today, or, an existing positive belief that served me today:

_____

_____

_____

MY GRATITUDES FOR TODAY
Today, I am grateful for:

_____

_____

_____

MY PLAN FOR TOMORROW
Tomorrow, I will end the day having done this important thing:

_____

_____

DATE: _____

MY "HAVE-DONE-LIST" FOR TODAY
I accomplished this today:

_____

_____

_____

I took this step towards my goal:

_____

_____

_____

MY "HAVE-BEEN-LIST" FOR TODAY
Here is a positive emotion I chose to feel today:

_____

_____

_____

Here is a new positive belief I chose to create today, or, an existing positive belief that served me today:

_____

_____

_____

MY GRATITUDES FOR TODAY
Today, I am grateful for:

_____

_____

_____

MY PLAN FOR TOMORROW
Tomorrow, I will end the day having done this important thing:

_____

_____

DATE: _____

MY "HAVE-DONE-LIST" FOR TODAY
I accomplished this today:

_____

_____

_____

I took this step towards my goal:

_____

_____

_____

MY "HAVE-BEEN-LIST" FOR TODAY
Here is a positive emotion I chose to feel today:

_____

_____

_____

Here is a new positive belief I chose to create today, or, an existing positive belief that served me today:

_____

_____

_____

MY GRATITUDES FOR TODAY
Today, I am grateful for:

_____

_____

_____

MY PLAN FOR TOMORROW
Tomorrow, I will end the day having done this important thing:

_____

_____

DATE: _____

MY "HAVE-DONE-LIST" FOR TODAY
I accomplished this today:

_____

_____

_____

I took this step towards my goal:

_____

_____

_____

MY "HAVE-BEEN-LIST" FOR TODAY
Here is a positive emotion I chose to feel today:

_____

_____

_____

Here is a new positive belief I chose to create today, or, an existing positive belief that served me today:

_____

_____

_____

MY GRATITUDES FOR TODAY
Today, I am grateful for:

_____

_____

_____

MY PLAN FOR TOMORROW
Tomorrow, I will end the day having done this important thing:

_____

_____

DATE: _____

MY "HAVE-DONE-LIST" FOR TODAY
I accomplished this today:

_____

_____

_____

I took this step towards my goal:

_____

_____

_____

MY "HAVE-BEEN-LIST" FOR TODAY
Here is a positive emotion I chose to feel today:

_____

_____

_____

Here is a new positive belief I chose to create today, or, an existing positive belief that served me today:

_____

_____

_____

MY GRATITUDES FOR TODAY
Today, I am grateful for:

_____

_____

_____

MY PLAN FOR TOMORROW
Tomorrow, I will end the day having done this important thing:

_____

_____

DATE: _____

MY "HAVE-DONE-LIST" FOR TODAY
I accomplished this today:

_____

_____

_____

I took this step towards my goal:

_____

_____

_____

MY "HAVE-BEEN-LIST" FOR TODAY
Here is a positive emotion I chose to feel today:

_____

_____

_____

Here is a new positive belief I chose to create today, or, an existing positive belief that served me today:

_____

_____

_____

MY GRATITUDES FOR TODAY
Today, I am grateful for:

_____

_____

_____

MY PLAN FOR TOMORROW
Tomorrow, I will end the day having done this important thing:

_____

_____

DATE: _____

MY "HAVE-DONE-LIST" FOR TODAY
I accomplished this today:

_____

_____

_____

I took this step towards my goal:

_____

_____

_____

MY "HAVE-BEEN-LIST" FOR TODAY
Here is a positive emotion I chose to feel today:

_____

_____

_____

Here is a new positive belief I chose to create today, or, an existing positive belief that served me today:

_____

_____

_____

MY GRATITUDES FOR TODAY
Today, I am grateful for:

_____

_____

_____

MY PLAN FOR TOMORROW
Tomorrow, I will end the day having done this important thing:

_____

_____

DATE: _____

MY "HAVE-DONE-LIST" FOR TODAY
I accomplished this today:

_____

_____

_____

I took this step towards my goal:

_____

_____

_____

MY "HAVE-BEEN-LIST" FOR TODAY
Here is a positive emotion I chose to feel today:

_____

_____

_____

Here is a new positive belief I chose to create today, or, an existing positive belief that served me today:

_____

_____

_____

MY GRATITUDES FOR TODAY
Today, I am grateful for:

_____

_____

_____

MY PLAN FOR TOMORROW
Tomorrow, I will end the day having done this important thing:

_____

_____

DATE: _____

MY "HAVE-DONE-LIST" FOR TODAY
I accomplished this today:

_____

_____

_____

I took this step towards my goal:

_____

_____

_____

MY "HAVE-BEEN-LIST" FOR TODAY
Here is a positive emotion I chose to feel today:

_____

_____

_____

Here is a new positive belief I chose to create today, or, an existing positive belief that served me today:

_____

_____

_____

MY GRATITUDES FOR TODAY
Today, I am grateful for:

_____

_____

_____

MY PLAN FOR TOMORROW
Tomorrow, I will end the day having done this important thing:

_____

_____

DATE: _____

MY "HAVE-DONE-LIST" FOR TODAY
I accomplished this today:

_____

_____

_____

I took this step towards my goal:

_____

_____

_____

MY "HAVE-BEEN-LIST" FOR TODAY
Here is a positive emotion I chose to feel today:

_____

_____

_____

Here is a new positive belief I chose to create today, or, an existing positive belief that served me today:

_____

_____

_____

MY GRATITUDES FOR TODAY
Today, I am grateful for:

_____

_____

_____

MY PLAN FOR TOMORROW
Tomorrow, I will end the day having done this important thing:

_____

_____

DATE: _____

MY "HAVE-DONE-LIST" FOR TODAY
I accomplished this today:

_____

_____

_____

I took this step towards my goal:

_____

_____

_____

MY "HAVE-BEEN-LIST" FOR TODAY
Here is a positive emotion I chose to feel today:

_____

_____

_____

Here is a new positive belief I chose to create today, or, an existing positive belief that served me today:

_____

_____

_____

MY GRATITUDES FOR TODAY
Today, I am grateful for:

_____

_____

_____

MY PLAN FOR TOMORROW
Tomorrow, I will end the day having done this important thing:

_____

_____

DATE: _____

MY "HAVE-DONE-LIST" FOR TODAY
I accomplished this today:

_____

_____

_____

I took this step towards my goal:

_____

_____

_____

MY "HAVE-BEEN-LIST" FOR TODAY
Here is a positive emotion I chose to feel today:

_____

_____

_____

Here is a new positive belief I chose to create today, or, an existing positive belief that served me today:

_____

_____

_____

MY GRATITUDES FOR TODAY
Today, I am grateful for:

_____

_____

_____

MY PLAN FOR TOMORROW
Tomorrow, I will end the day having done this important thing:

_____

_____

DATE: _____

MY "HAVE-DONE-LIST" FOR TODAY
I accomplished this today:

_____

_____

_____

I took this step towards my goal:

_____

_____

_____

MY "HAVE-BEEN-LIST" FOR TODAY
Here is a positive emotion I chose to feel today:

_____

_____

_____

Here is a new positive belief I chose to create today, or, an existing positive belief that served me today:

_____

_____

_____

MY GRATITUDES FOR TODAY
Today, I am grateful for:

_____

_____

_____

MY PLAN FOR TOMORROW
Tomorrow, I will end the day having done this important thing:

_____

_____

DATE: _____

MY "HAVE-DONE-LIST" FOR TODAY
I accomplished this today:

_____

_____

_____

I took this step towards my goal:

_____

_____

_____

MY "HAVE-BEEN-LIST" FOR TODAY
Here is a positive emotion I chose to feel today:

_____

_____

_____

Here is a new positive belief I chose to create today, or, an existing positive belief that served me today:

_____

_____

_____

MY GRATITUDES FOR TODAY
Today, I am grateful for:

_____

_____

_____

MY PLAN FOR TOMORROW
Tomorrow, I will end the day having done this important thing:

_____

_____

DATE: _____

MY "HAVE-DONE-LIST" FOR TODAY
I accomplished this today:

_____

_____

_____

I took this step towards my goal:

_____

_____

_____

MY "HAVE-BEEN-LIST" FOR TODAY
Here is a positive emotion I chose to feel today:

_____

_____

_____

Here is a new positive belief I chose to create today, or, an existing positive belief that served me today:

_____

_____

_____

MY GRATITUDES FOR TODAY
Today, I am grateful for:

_____

_____

_____

MY PLAN FOR TOMORROW
Tomorrow, I will end the day having done this important thing:

_____

_____

DATE: _____

MY "HAVE-DONE-LIST" FOR TODAY
I accomplished this today:

_____

_____

_____

I took this step towards my goal:

_____

_____

_____

MY "HAVE-BEEN-LIST" FOR TODAY
Here is a positive emotion I chose to feel today:

_____

_____

_____

Here is a new positive belief I chose to create today, or, an existing positive belief that served me today:

_____

_____

_____

MY GRATITUDES FOR TODAY
Today, I am grateful for:

_____

_____

_____

MY PLAN FOR TOMORROW
Tomorrow, I will end the day having done this important thing:

_____

_____

DATE: _____

MY "HAVE-DONE-LIST" FOR TODAY
I accomplished this today:

_____

_____

_____

I took this step towards my goal:

_____

_____

_____

MY "HAVE-BEEN-LIST" FOR TODAY
Here is a positive emotion I chose to feel today:

_____

_____

_____

Here is a new positive belief I chose to create today, or, an existing positive belief that served me today:

_____

_____

_____

MY GRATITUDES FOR TODAY
Today, I am grateful for:

_____

_____

_____

MY PLAN FOR TOMORROW
Tomorrow, I will end the day having done this important thing:

_____

_____

DATE: _____

MY "HAVE-DONE-LIST" FOR TODAY
I accomplished this today:

_____

_____

_____

I took this step towards my goal:

_____

_____

_____

MY "HAVE-BEEN-LIST" FOR TODAY
Here is a positive emotion I chose to feel today:

_____

_____

_____

Here is a new positive belief I chose to create today, or, an existing positive belief that served me today:

_____

_____

_____

MY GRATITUDES FOR TODAY
Today, I am grateful for:

_____

_____

_____

MY PLAN FOR TOMORROW
Tomorrow, I will end the day having done this important thing:

_____

_____

DATE: _____

MY "HAVE-DONE-LIST" FOR TODAY
I accomplished this today:

_____

_____

_____

I took this step towards my goal:

_____

_____

_____

MY "HAVE-BEEN-LIST" FOR TODAY
Here is a positive emotion I chose to feel today:

_____

_____

_____

Here is a new positive belief I chose to create today, or, an existing positive belief that served me today:

_____

_____

_____

MY GRATITUDES FOR TODAY
Today, I am grateful for:

_____

_____

_____

MY PLAN FOR TOMORROW
Tomorrow, I will end the day having done this important thing:

_____

_____

DATE: _____

MY "HAVE-DONE-LIST" FOR TODAY
I accomplished this today:

_____

_____

_____

I took this step towards my goal:

_____

_____

_____

MY "HAVE-BEEN-LIST" FOR TODAY
Here is a positive emotion I chose to feel today:

_____

_____

_____

Here is a new positive belief I chose to create today, or, an existing positive belief that served me today:

_____

_____

_____

MY GRATITUDES FOR TODAY
Today, I am grateful for:

_____

_____

_____

MY PLAN FOR TOMORROW
Tomorrow, I will end the day having done this important thing:

_____

_____

DATE: _____

MY "HAVE-DONE-LIST" FOR TODAY
I accomplished this today:

_____

_____

_____

I took this step towards my goal:

_____

_____

_____

MY "HAVE-BEEN-LIST" FOR TODAY
Here is a positive emotion I chose to feel today:

_____

_____

_____

Here is a new positive belief I chose to create today, or, an existing positive belief that served me today:

_____

_____

_____

MY GRATITUDES FOR TODAY
Today, I am grateful for:

_____

_____

_____

MY PLAN FOR TOMORROW
Tomorrow, I will end the day having done this important thing:

_____

_____

DATE: _____

MY "HAVE-DONE-LIST" FOR TODAY
I accomplished this today:

_____

_____

_____

I took this step towards my goal:

_____

_____

_____

MY "HAVE-BEEN-LIST" FOR TODAY
Here is a positive emotion I chose to feel today:

_____

_____

_____

Here is a new positive belief I chose to create today, or, an existing positive belief that served me today:

_____

_____

_____

MY GRATITUDES FOR TODAY
Today, I am grateful for:

_____

_____

_____

MY PLAN FOR TOMORROW
Tomorrow, I will end the day having done this important thing:

_____

_____

DATE: _____

MY "HAVE-DONE-LIST" FOR TODAY
I accomplished this today:

_____

_____

_____

I took this step towards my goal:

_____

_____

_____

MY "HAVE-BEEN-LIST" FOR TODAY
Here is a positive emotion I chose to feel today:

_____

_____

_____

Here is a new positive belief I chose to create today, or, an existing positive belief that served me today:

_____

_____

_____

MY GRATITUDES FOR TODAY
Today, I am grateful for:

_____

_____

_____

MY PLAN FOR TOMORROW
Tomorrow, I will end the day having done this important thing:

_____

_____

DATE: _____

MY "HAVE-DONE-LIST" FOR TODAY
I accomplished this today:

_____

_____

_____

I took this step towards my goal:

_____

_____

_____

MY "HAVE-BEEN-LIST" FOR TODAY
Here is a positive emotion I chose to feel today:

_____

_____

_____

Here is a new positive belief I chose to create today, or, an existing positive belief that served me today:

_____

_____

_____

MY GRATITUDES FOR TODAY
Today, I am grateful for:

_____

_____

_____

MY PLAN FOR TOMORROW
Tomorrow, I will end the day having done this important thing:

_____

_____

DATE: _____

MY "HAVE-DONE-LIST" FOR TODAY
I accomplished this today:

_____

_____

_____

I took this step towards my goal:

_____

_____

_____

MY "HAVE-BEEN-LIST" FOR TODAY
Here is a positive emotion I chose to feel today:

_____

_____

_____

Here is a new positive belief I chose to create today, or, an existing positive belief that served me today:

_____

_____

_____

MY GRATITUDES FOR TODAY
Today, I am grateful for:

_____

_____

_____

MY PLAN FOR TOMORROW
Tomorrow, I will end the day having done this important thing:

_____

_____

DATE: _____

MY "HAVE-DONE-LIST" FOR TODAY
I accomplished this today:

_____

_____

_____

I took this step towards my goal:

_____

_____

_____

MY "HAVE-BEEN-LIST" FOR TODAY
Here is a positive emotion I chose to feel today:

_____

_____

_____

Here is a new positive belief I chose to create today, or, an existing positive belief that served me today:

_____

_____

_____

MY GRATITUDES FOR TODAY
Today, I am grateful for:

_____

_____

_____

MY PLAN FOR TOMORROW
Tomorrow, I will end the day having done this important thing:

_____

_____

DATE: _____

MY "HAVE-DONE-LIST" FOR TODAY
I accomplished this today:

_____

_____

_____

I took this step towards my goal:

_____

_____

_____

MY "HAVE-BEEN-LIST" FOR TODAY
Here is a positive emotion I chose to feel today:

_____

_____

_____

Here is a new positive belief I chose to create today, or, an existing positive belief that served me today:

_____

_____

_____

MY GRATITUDES FOR TODAY
Today, I am grateful for:

_____

_____

_____

MY PLAN FOR TOMORROW
Tomorrow, I will end the day having done this important thing:

_____

_____

MY "HAVE-DONE-LIST" FOR TODAY
I accomplished this today:

_____

_____

_____

I took this step towards my goal:

_____

_____

_____

MY "HAVE-BEEN-LIST" FOR TODAY
Here is a positive emotion I chose to feel today:

_____

_____

_____

Here is a new positive belief I chose to create today, or, an existing positive belief that served me today:

_____

_____

_____

MY GRATITUDES FOR TODAY
Today, I am grateful for:

_____

_____

_____

MY PLAN FOR TOMORROW
Tomorrow, I will end the day having done this important thing:

_____

_____

ABOUT THE AUTHOR

NATHALIE PLAMONDON-THOMAS

The Expert with a proven system to reprogram your brain and give you transformational results. Founder of the THINK Yourself® ACADEMY, speaker, Master Life Coach and No.1 best-selling author of seven books on wellness and empowerment. Nathalie combines over 25 years of experience in sales and over 30 years in the fitness industry. In 2007, Goodlife Fitness named her "Fitness Instructor of the Year" for Canada. She uses the principles of neuroscience and brain reprogramming in her practice as a Life Coach and Master Practitioner in NLP.

She retrains your brain to end self-sabotage and live your full potential.

"You can take a horse to water, but you can't make him drink".

Somehow, Nathalie can.

"Hi, I'm Nathalie.

My parents were freaks!!!

They never put a gate by the stairs when my brother and I were babies because they never wanted to imply that we could fall. They would say: "Be careful around there;" they didn't say: "Don't fall". If they needed me to bring a full glass of water to the table they would just say: "Use a strong firm hand and bring this glass to the table," instead of creating anxiety around the action of carrying the water by saying: "Don't spill it!"

There were signs everywhere in the house with motivational phrases like: "You can be everything you want"; "Yes you can"; "You will miss 100% of the shots you won't take"; "If you're going to do it, do it right", etc.

On Sundays, we didn't go to church (although we are Christian Catholics). Instead, my parents would make us sit in the living room to listen to motivational tape cassettes from Jean-Marc Chaput, Zig Ziglar, Og Mandino, etc. Needless to say, I was brainwashed into positive thinking at a very young age.

I believe that my life purpose is to motivate, inspire and support people to discover that they have everything inside themselves in order to be their best and live to their full potential.

I got my first 'calling' to help people at a very young age. My parents would not read us Disney stories at night. They would either sing us a song to put us to sleep with their guitar (which explains my love for music), or they would tell us motivational stories. Here is my favourite bedtime story: It is about an old man on the beach, who was throwing starfish back into the sea, one by one. A little girl asked him: "What are you doing sir?" and the old man responded: "I am saving the starfish from dying, as the tide brought them to shore, they will dry and die if I don't throw them back in the sea."

The little girl looked at the endlessly long beach and said: "But sir, no offence, but there are so many, you can't save them all! It doesn't really make a difference."

The old man responded, as he was showing the little girl the starfish that he was holding in his hands: "Well my dear, for this particular starfish, it makes a whole world of difference."

I was thinking: "When I grow up, I will be a starfish saviour and save them all, one at a time!" And the rest is history.

I was born in Saint-Raymond, a small town near Quebec City, Canada. I lived in Quebec for a big chunk of my life as a successful entrepreneur in the printing industry, with over 50 employees, mastering human resources and sales techniques until I moved to Toronto, Ontario in my twenties, where I got seriously into fitness, personal training and nutrition consultation all while accumulating 16 more years of experience in sales in the natural food industry.

After reaching the top of my game as the No.1 Fitness Instructor in Canada, I realized that being my own personal best wasn't fulfilling me. I started to realize that even though I was helping people, my clients were not successful because I was giving them a better kale salad recipe or showing them a different way of doing push-ups. They thrived because they were changing the way they thought. Their mindset was influenced by mine.

I then started to study neuroscience and the astonishing powers of the brain. I got a Neuro-Linguistic Programming (NLP) Master certification and Life Coaching certifications and have spent the last 10 years developing a system combining my experience as an entrepreneur, my health and wellness knowledge and the specific processes I use with the thousands of clients I have helped to reach their full potential.

I work with clients one-on-one and propel people into the life they want through my coaching, books, events and speaking engagements. I also continue to teach fitness classes, 30 years and counting, using fitness as an introductory platform in order to help people be their best.

Eight years ago, I also started to work with kids in schools, which gives me even more opportunity to impact and improve people's lives as I believe if certain values are planted at a young age, flourishing happens sooner in life.

I now live in White Rock, British Columbia with my loving husband Duff and we are celebrating our 15th anniversary this year."

NATHALIE P.
Transformation Expert
Master Coach - No. 1 Best Selling
Author - Speaker

www.thinkyourself.com

From the same author:
THINK Yourself® THIN
THINK Yourself® SUCCESSFUL
THINK Yourself® HEALTHY
THINK Yourself® CLEAN from the inside out
WHEN YOU'RE HUNGRY YOU GOTTA EAT
QUAND ON A FAIM, IL FAUT MANGER
SHINE
SIMPLE SUCCESS STRATEGIES

All available at: ww.thinkyourself.com and www.amazon.com
and www.amazon.ca